DO TRY THIS AT HOME
COOK IT!

The Punk Science team lives and works in the Science Museum. They spend their days performing experiments of all shapes and sizes and on the odd occasion performing science shows.

The Punk Scientists are: Jon Milton, the fearless and clueless leader of the team. He's always ready with a plan – it's not always a good one but it is a plan nonetheless. He likes experiments that help him with his hobbies of flying and scuba diving. By hobbies we actually mean things he'd like to do if he wasn't so lazy.

Brad Gross is the number-one American on the Punk Science team, and that has nothing to do with him being the only American on the Punk Science team. When Brad isn't doing experiments he's drumming, and when he's not drumming he's talking, and when he's not talking he's experimenting, and when he's not experimenting he's drumming, and so on. It's very much a drum, talk, experiment cycle. Brad is living proof that science isn't just for clever people.

Last and certainly not least is Dan Carter Hope. In Dan's head he is the ultimate guitar-playing action hero. Unfortunately for him his action-hero status doesn't go any further than his head – not even a little bit into his neck. However, his guitar playing does stretch a little further although it does seem to fall short of his fingers. This doesn't stop him from performing exciting experiments, it just makes it really difficult to see what he's doing, because most of the time he's too afraid to look.

Other books

Macmillan Children's Books is delighted to be publishing the following **brilliant** books in association with the Science Museum.

Do Try This At Home!
28 spectacular experiments for scientists of all ages
Jon Milton

Why Is Snot Green?
And other extremely important questions
(and answers) from the Science Museum
Glenn Murphy

How Loud Can You Burp?
And other extremely important questions
(and answers) from the Science Museum
Glenn Murphy

Stuff That Scares Your Pants Off!
The Science Museum Book of Scary Things (and ways to avoid them)
Glenn Murphy

Does Farting Make You Faster?
And other extremely important questions (and answers)
about sport from the Science Museum
Glenn Murphy

Will Farts Destroy the Planet?
And other extremely important questions (and answers)
about climate change from the Science Museum
Glenn Murphy

DO TRY THIS AT HOME

COOK IT!

30 yummy recipes for scientists of all ages

By Jon Milton

Photographs by Stuart Cox

Macmillan Children's Books

This book is produced in association with the Science Museum. Sales of this book support the Science Museum's exhibitions and programmes.

Internationally recognised as one of the world's leading science centres, the Science Museum, London, contains more than 10,000 amazing exhibits, two fantastic simulator rides and the astounding IMAX cinema. Enter a world of discovery and achievement, where you can see, touch and experience real objects and icons which have shaped the world we live in today or visit www.sciencemuseum.org.uk to find out more.

Thanks to Deborah Bloxam, Stuart Cox, Tracey Ridgewell, Rachel Vale, Dan Newman, Gaby Morgan, Evie Weston, and the Bloxam family – Richard, Annie, William, Eddie, Florrie and Oscar – for the use of their beautiful house.

First published 2011 by Macmillan Children's Books

This edition published 2013 by Macmillan Children's Books
a division of Macmillan Publishers Limited
20 New Wharf Road, London N1 9RR
Basingstoke and Oxford
Associated companies throughout the world
www.panmacmillan.com

ISBN 978-1-4472-0553-1

A CIP catalogue record for this book is available from the British Library.

Typeset by Perfect Bound Ltd
Printed and bound in China

Contents

Introduction

At Punk Science HQ, at the Science Museum, we love doing experiments, but all that experimenting can make you quite hungry and we didn't want to stop experimenting to cook food. Eventually, when we were really very hungry indeed, we realized that cooking is a lot like doing experiments. When we cook, we can learn about science at the same time, but best of all we get to eat the results. So let's get started.

First off we will give you some tips about cooking and how to find your way around the kitchen. Believe us, that is trickier than it sounds. When we started, we didn't even know where the kitchen was. We looked for ages, found what we thought was a kitchen, started cooking, then suddenly a man came in shouting, 'What are you doing in my toilet?' Needless to say, we didn't eat what we had made.

There are lots of bits of useful information that will come in handy dotted throughout this book. Have a flick through and see for yourself, but try to keep a bit of space in your brain so you can follow all the delicious recipes that we have put together in the Punk Science Kitchen of Power . . . (It's really just called the Punk Science Kitchen, but we thought it makes it sound a bit more exciting if we call it the Punk Science Kitchen of Power.) And alongside our easy-to-follow, step-by-step recipes, which we cooked all by ourselves, with no help whatsoever, we've also got some experiments, which you can't eat, but you can do with food. All of this is marvellous and it's very nice of you to be reading this bit and all, but aren't you getting a bit hungry? Because we're famished. So let's get going.

READ THIS!

Cooking is great fun, but it can be a tad dangerous too. Ovens, knives, hobs and blenders are useful tools to help you get the job done, but they can be pretty nasty if you aren't careful around them and don't treat them with respect. Trust us – we have just little cuts and mild burns and they really, really hurt. In fact, they hurt so much it made us cry, so you must promise to be careful. We will help you, and of course your grown-up helper will assist you too. Oh, by the way, we meant it about the promise, so repeat after us:

I promise to be safe with all things sharp and all things hot. OK, that's good enough for us, but you'd better keep your promise or there'll be trouble.

Dangerous tools aren't the only things you need to be careful about in the kitchen. You also have to watch out for germs and bacteria, which is particularly tricky because you can't see them, and not because they're wearing hats and moustaches as disguises – it's because they are really, really small. Some germs aren't bad, but some of them can be really nasty to us and make us really ill. So the best way to stop the sneaky so-and-sos is by washing your hands before you start cooking and after you have handled raw meat, fish or eggs. You will also need to wash fruit and veg before you use it and make sure your kitchen is kept nice and clean, otherwise it could result in everyone who's eaten your lovely food needing a rapid visit to the loo, and not just to have a look around to see if the taps work, if you know what we mean.

We've also tried to help you out by using these rather handy warnings and ratings throughout the book . . .

Warnings and Ratings

Hot Stuff
This shows when you'll be using things that get hot, like ovens and hobs. Use oven gloves whenever you're taking anything hot out of the oven.

Grown-up Helper
You'll probably need a grown-up around for most things, but this shows where they'll need to do something for you.

That's a different kind of hot, Dan

Difficulty
5 This shows you how hard the recipe is likely to be on a scale of one to five, one being easy.

Time
45 mins This shows how long it will take – pretty obvious, really.

Make sure your grown-up helper is vaguely mature . . .

Cooking Words
As you need to understand certain cooking-related words in order to follow a recipe, we've given a helpful list of some of these on pages 84–85.

Jon doing something very difficult . . .

Leek and Potato Soup

This makes enough for four people,
or two if you like a big bowl.

No, not a leak, a leek

What You'll Need

- 3 leeks
- 1 large potato or 2 middle-sized ones
- 30g butter
- 500ml chicken or vegetable stock (follow the instructions on your packet to see how to make this)
- Salt and freshly ground black pepper

Equipment

- A sharp knife for chopping
- A chopping board
- A colander
- A peeler (optional)
- A large saucepan
- A measuring jug
- A blender

Why did the orange juice break up with the milk?
The relationship had turned sour.

Soup is all about choices. For example, you can have soup as a starter or on its own; you can put loads of different vegetables in, or meat or cheese or even pasta. But for this one we're going to take a leek.

No, not a leak, a leek. It's a vegetable from the onion family and a national symbol of Wales. The most important thing about leeks is that they are extremely tasty in soups.

1. Cut the tops, including any dark green leaves, off the leeks and put them in the composter or the bin. Put the leeks in a colander and wash well, making sure you get rid of any dirt that might be hidden in the leeky layers at the end, then chop them up. Peel and dice the spuds, cutting large potatoes into about 12 chunks.

2. Pop the butter in the pan over a medium heat. When it starts to melt, add the chopped leeks and spuds and cook them for around five minutes, stirring occasionally.

3. Add the stock and bring it to the boil, then cover the pan and turn the heat down so it simmers gently for 20 minutes or until the potatoes are tender.

4. Switch off the heat and let the soup cool down a bit. Then carefully ladle it into a blender and blend until smooth. You might need help with this bit as blenders can be a bit tricky; just look how confused Brad is, above.

5. You might want to warm your soup up a bit before you eat it, and season it once you've tasted it (this means adding salt and pepper). For some reason, Brad likes his soup a bit cold, which is odd, but, then again, so is he.

If You Liked That, Try This

- Use more or less stock to make a thinner or thicker soup.
- You can make an even healthier soup if you scrub the potatoes but don't peel them, but your soup won't look as nice.
- If you put this soup in the fridge and serve it chilled, it's called vichyssoise. Try it with a spoon of cream swirled in for a very posh summer starter.

Boiled, Fried and Poached Eggs

What came first, the chicken or the egg? Well, if all chickens look like the one on the right, let's hope it's the egg. Here are three ways to cook eggs.

I wouldn't eat those eggs . . .

What You'll Need
- Eggs – 1 per recipe, or more if you like
- 1 tablespoon sunflower oil (fried)
- 1 teaspoon vinegar (poached)
- Bread for toast – as much as you want
- Butter

Equipment

Boiled
- A small saucepan
- A spoon

Fried
- A frying pan
- A fish slice (also called a metal spatula)

Poached
- A small bowl
- A wooden spoon
- A slotted spoon (one with holes in)

Boiled Egg

1. Fill a saucepan three-quarters full of water and bring it to the boil. Then take a spoon, pop your egg on it and then carefully put your egg into the pan of water. Leave your egg in the pan for four minutes for a runny egg or five minutes if you like a less runny egg (eight minutes will give you a hard-boiled egg). Then use your spoon to take the egg out.

2. Cut the top off the egg and dunk in some toast soldiers. Not real soldiers though – they won't like it.

If you want salt and pepper, sprinkle it on the soldiers, not the egg!

Fried Egg

1. Put the oil in the frying pan and heat it up on a medium heat.

2. Crack the egg into a cup and pour it gently into the pan.

3. Cook for about four minutes and then serve it up, maybe on a bit of toast, and eat it straight away.

Why is cream so fed up?
Because it's always being whipped!

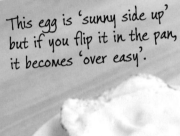

This egg is 'sunny side up' but if you flip it in the pan, it becomes 'over easy'.

Good egg   Eggy breath   Egghead

The Science Bit

Eggs are a good source of useful stuff your body needs:
protein
vitamin D
vitamin A
vitamin B2
iodine
When you cook an egg, its proteins change. So instead of being little curled-up proteins just doing their own thing, they become a big chain of joined-up proteins. The longer you cook an egg for, the more bonds are formed. This is what makes it hard, like in a hard-boiled egg.

Poached Egg

1. This one is a bit trickier. Start the same way as for a boiled egg to begin with. Boil water in a saucepan, but then add a little vinegar to the water and turn the heat down so the water's not bubbling.

2. Crack the egg into a small bowl.

3. With a wooden spoon, swirl the water gently so it looks like a whirlpool. Be careful not to splash the water out over you. Remember, it is very hot. Get a grown-up to help you with this bit, if you like.

4. Pour the egg gently from the bowl into the middle of the swirling water. It might go a bit frothy, but don't worry. Leave it for four minutes for a runny egg and longer for a firmer one . . . eggsellent.

5. Take the egg out of the water using a slotted spoon to drain all the water away. Serve straight away, maybe on a bit of toast.

Cheese on Toast with a Twist

This is hot, tasty food for lazy people like us. We usually have at least two each. You can choose your favourite toppings. You can have cheese and tomato like Dan; tuna, cheese and sweetcorn like Jon or cheese and ham like Brad, or whatever you fancy. Except ice cream and jelly – that would be silly.

The Science Bit

Have you ever wondered what happens to cheese when it melts? With a hard cheese like Cheddar, first the milk fat melts, which makes it more supple. Then, at higher temperatures, the protein bonds break and it becomes a thick liquid. Try melting different cheeses and see what happens to them. Cheddar goes gloopy, brie becomes a thinner liquid and mozzarella goes all stringy and stretchy. Yum!

What You'll Need
- 1 slice of bread per toastie – wholemeal or white

Toppings such as:
- Cheddar cheese
- A few slices of ham
- Half a can of tuna
- Half a can of sweetcorn
- Slices of tomato

Equipment
- A grill
- A grater
- A knife
- A chopping board
- Small bowls for your toppings
- A knife for spreading
- Spoons for dolloping and mixing
- A toaster (optional)

1. Preheat the grill to medium. This means switch it on so it's ready to use when you're ready to use it.

2. Prepare your toppings. Grating cheese can be grating and leave you cheesed off. Not Jon though – he loves it.

3. Our little tip is to toast the bread a bit first so that the bread is crispy on both sides.

4. Pop your toppings of choice on the lightly toasted bread. Place the tomato slices perfectly, otherwise there will be absolute chaos. (There won't really be chaos. Plonk it on however you like – just don't tell Dan.)

5. Place your cheese on toast under a medium grill for about five minutes. Make sure you keep an eye on it or it might burn, and that would be pants!

Baked Potato

Not-too-hot-to-handle
hot potatoes.

Equipment
- A baking tray
- A fork
- Spoons, bowls, knives etc. for your filling
- Knives for your butter and for cutting open the spud

What You'll Need
- 1 large baking potato per person
- Butter
- Filling of choice. We've gone for baked beans, chilli and cheese – but not all together. For the chilli, we adapted the punkognese sauce on page 25 by making it without the basil and adding half a teaspoon of mild chilli powder and a can of kidney beans five minutes before the end.

When something is a bit difficult to handle, people sometimes say it's a hot potato. Well, these hot potatoes aren't hot potatoes in that sense, if you get what we mean . . . they're just potatoes that are hot. They're really easy to cook, but you will have to do a lot of waiting around. Fortunately, we're extremely good at waiting around for food.

1. Put the baking tray in the oven and put it on at 220°C/gas mark 7. Then wash and dry your spud and prick it with a fork several times so that steam can get out without the potato exploding. Place the potato on the hot baking tray and leave it in the oven for one and a quarter hours.

2. While you're waiting, prepare your filling of choice.

Waiting . . .

Still waiting . . .

The Science Bit

Baking potatoes have lots of starch in their cells, which swells when it's cooked and makes the potato all fluffy and delicious.

STILL waiting . . .

Microwave Magic

If you don't want to wait, you can use a microwave to cook your potato. It does this by making the water molecules in the potato jiggle about, getting them all excited and hot. BUT a microwave doesn't dry the potato skin, making it all nice and crispy like you get in the oven. Waiting or soggy skin? You decide! Or enjoy the best of both worlds by starting it off in the microwave and crisping it up in the oven.

3. That's enough waiting. Now it's time to get your potato out of the oven, cut it open and put in your filling. You can see what we chose, but you can put in whatever you want – except that, or that, or that other thing you're thinking of.

Keep your parents happy, put something green next to the potato!

Dips and Dippers

Time to go a bit dippy for our delicious and easy-to-make dips and get stuck in with our lovely dippers, to be dipped in the dips.

You don't have to make all of them!

Equipment
- A tin opener
- Knives for chopping
- A chopping board
- Spoons or forks for mixing
- A garlic crusher or small grater
- A small bowl for each dip you make

Dip 1
Speedy Salsa

- 1 400g can of chopped tomatoes
- A generous squeeze of ketchup
- 1 small onion, chopped

1. Mix with a fork or spoon.

Chilli Cheat

When you chop a chilli, hold it on the cutting board with a fork so you don't have to touch it with your fingers. Scrape it from the board straight into the dish, then wash the board and knife. Touching a cut chilli and then rubbing your eye (or picking your nose) can REALLY hurt! The seeds are the hottest part, so scrape these out and just use the flesh if you don't want it too spicy.

Dip 2
Coriander Quickie

- 4 tablespoons Greek yogurt
- A handful of fresh coriander, chopped

1. Stir the coriander into the Greek yogurt.

Hey, don't use your fingers to dip!

Dip 3
Express Avocado

- 1 ripe avocado
- 1 clove garlic
- Optional extras: chilli powder or finely chopped chilli; lemon or lime juice; finely chopped onion; salt; fresh coriander

1. Mash the avocado, crush or grate the garlic and mix all ingredients together.

The Science Bit

The hotness of chillies is measured in Scoville units, invented by a chemist called Wilbur Scoville around 1912. The hottest chilli in the world is the aji, which measures 30,000–50,000 Scovilles. Compare that with a normal red pepper, which measures 0–600 Scovilles. Ouch!

No, you can use your fingers to HOLD the dippers.

Dippers
- Carrots, celery and peppers (red, yellow or orange), chopped into sticks
- Breadsticks
- Tortilla chips

Dip 4
Heavenly
Homemade Houmous
- Half a can of chickpeas
- 1 tablespoon olive oil
- Juice of half a lemon, or 2 teaspoons lemon juice
- Optional extras: 1 clove of garlic, crushed or grated; 2 tablespoons of tahini (sesame-seed paste you can buy in jars in supermarkets)

1. Mash the chickpeas as smooth or lumpy as you like and mix in the other ingredients. Add some water, a tablespoon at a time, if you want it less thick.

There you go — easy isn't it?

17

Tuna Salad

Makes enough for four people

What You'll Need

- 50g lettuce
- 50g spinach
- 50g rocket
- Half a cucumber
- 3 tomatoes
- 2 carrots
- 1 stick of celery
- 1 red or yellow pepper
- 1 small can of tuna

For the dressing:

- 30ml olive oil
- 10ml balsamic vinegar

Equipment

- Knives for chopping
- A chopping board
- A salad bowl
- A tin opener
- Big spoons for mixing and serving
- A sealable jar

Salad is tasty and healthy stuff, and super-easy to make. If you don't like or don't have any of the stuff we've used, you don't have to put it in yours, and if there's any other stuff you like, feel free to add it. Last time we made this, we found we had some amazing purple radishes, so we put them in too.

If you cut everything into similar-sized chunks, your salad will mix better. If some bits are much smaller than others, they'll end up at the bottom of the bowl.

1. Wash the veg and shake it so it's not too wet. Then tear the leaves, grate the carrots and chop everything else into bite-sized pieces.

2. Put everything into a large bowl and mix it together gently.

Lettuce Learn

Lettuce has been grown for thousands of years – both the Greeks and the Romans grew several varieties and ate them both cooked and raw in salads at the beginning or end of a meal. Tomatoes, on the other hand, only began to be imported to Europe relatively recently, in the fifteenth and sixteenth centuries.

3. To make the dressing, put the olive oil and balsamic vinegar in a jar and screw the top on carefully. Dan forgot, as you can see below. Once it is all shook up, pour over the salad and serve.

The Science Bit

You will notice that the oil and vinegar don't mix together at first. This is because they are different densities. When you shake the jar, you force them to mix by creating what's called an emulsion. An emulsion is made up of two or more liquids that don't normally mix but, as with our salad dressing, one of the liquids is broken up in the other so it looks like it's mixed when in fact they are still two separate liquids. It's just that one is in lots of tiny little bits dotted around the other.

If You Liked That, Try This

- You can make salad dressing in larger quantities and keep it in the jar in the fridge. Just give it another shake before you use it.
- Try adding other things to the dressing to change the flavour. Crushed garlic, a teaspoon of honey and a teaspoon of mustard, or chopped herbs all work well. Or try using different flavoured oils and vinegars.

Pizza

Get a punk pizza the action.

What You'll Need
For the sauce:
- 1 can chopped tomatoes
- 10ml olive oil
- 2 tablespoons tomato purée
- Basil (a few leaves, not some bloke)
- 1 teaspoon sugar
- Salt and freshly ground black pepper

For the dough:
- 100g self-raising flour, plus a bit extra for rolling out on
- 1 teaspoon baking powder
- 30ml milk
- A little drizzle of olive oil

Makes one medium pizza

Equipment
- A tin opener
- A sharp knife
- A chopping board
- A small saucepan
- A sieve
- A mixing bowl
- A wooden spoon
- A clean, flat surface
- A rolling pin
- A baking tray

TOP PIZZA TOPPINGS
Cheeses – mozzarella, Cheddar
Ham
Black olives
Tuna
Pepperoni
Mushrooms
Red pepper
Sweetcorn
Cooked chicken
Sliced tomatoes
Basil
Pineapple

To make the sauce:

1. Pour the olive oil into the saucepan and heat gently. Add the tomatoes and simmer gently for ten minutes. (This is a good time to get your pizza toppings ready.)

2. Tear the washed basil leaves into pieces and add to the tomatoes. Stir in the tomato purée and simmer for another five minutes.

3. Taste your sauce (be careful not to burn your tongue) and add a tiny bit of salt, pepper and sugar if you think it needs it. Once you're happy with the way it tastes, leave the sauce to cool while you make your dough.

Fact
Tomatoes are fruits, not vegetables, as they contain seeds.

To make the dough:

1. Preheat the oven to 200°C/gas mark 6.

2. Sift the flour and baking powder into a mixing bowl.

3. Pour in the milk and give it a mix, then add the olive oil and give it another mix.

4. When it's all sticking together and is quite soft, dust a little flour on to a rolling pin and on your clean work surface and put the dough on it.

5. Roll the dough out, but don't make it too thin. Try and roll it so that it's round, like a pizza is round.

6. Get some of your tomato sauce and carefully spoon a little on to the pizza dough. Use the spoon to smooth it out a bit, but don't press down.

7. Here's the fun part. You can top the pizza with whatever you want. You can put on cheese, ham and pineapple like Brad, or cheese, extra tomatoes, red peppers and basil like Jon, or mushrooms, cheese and red peppers like Dan, or whatever you choose.

8. Carefully transfer your pizza to a baking tray and put it into the oven for about twenty minutes. Remember to keep an eye on it so it doesn't burn.

The Science Bit

When flour is mixed with water (or milk) and made into a dough, protein molecules link up to form long gluten molecules. These are all coiled up and have lots of kinks, which is what makes the dough stretchy and elastic. Rolling the dough flat stretches the coils out, but they will spring back slightly when you stop rolling, which is why pizza dough is so springy!

Spaghetti Punkognese

Feeds four punks

What You'll Need
- 1 onion
- A clove of garlic
- 1 tablespoon olive oil
- 250g of minced beef or lamb (or a vegetarian alternative)
- 1 can of chopped tomatoes
- 1 carrot
- Basil (fresh is best)
- Salt and freshly ground black pepper
- 500g spaghetti (or a good handful if you can't be bothered to weigh it)
- Optional: grated Parmesan cheese

Equipment
- A sharp knife
- A chopping board
- A garlic crusher or small grater
- A medium saucepan with a lid
- A wooden spoon
- A fork or spoon
- A big saucepan
- A colander or big sieve

1. Chop your onion into little bits (see 'The Science Bit' opposite to see why this can make you cry and how to avoid that). Then peel the garlic clove and grate it or crush it in a garlic crusher. You've got to be pretty tough to do this, unlike Jon.

2. Pour a little bit of oil in a saucepan and put it on a medium heat. Wait a couple of minutes for the oil to warm up, then add the onion and garlic and stir for a few minutes until soft. Then put in the meat. Cook it until it changes to a brown colour, making sure

you stir it occasionally so all the meat is cooked.

3. Put in the tomatoes. You'll need to use a fork or a spoon to mush them up a bit. Half fill the empty tomato tin with water and pour it into the pan.

4. Chop the carrot into little bits. You can do this by slicing it in half lengthways, then halve those two bits lengthways again and then cut them into little bits widthways. Add the chopped carrots to the saucepan and stir again.

5. Put a lid on the pan and leave this on a low to medium heat for about 20

minutes. Give it a stir every now and again if you like.

6. While you're waiting for your sauce to cook, boil a large saucepan of water and stick in your spaghetti, but be careful not to boil your fingers at the same time. Use a fork to push the spaghetti down as it goes soft, to make sure it's all under the water. Cook it for about ten minutes, or according to the instructions on the packet.

7. Meanwhile, taste your sauce and put in a little salt and pepper if you want to and some basil (it can be the dried stuff but fresh is better).

8. When your spaghetti is cooked, drain it then plonk it on some plates and whack the sauce on top. Add some Parmesan if you want, and enjoy.

The Science Bit

There are a few bits of science going on here. First up, the onions. Onions don't make us cry because they bully us or call us names. Seriously, though, it's all to do with cutting them. When you cut an onion, you break cells, which releases sulphenic acids. These then mix with enzymes in the onion that weren't previously able to mix. This produces a mild sulphuric acid that gets caught in the air and travels up to your eyes, irritating them just enough to make you cry.

If you put your onions in the fridge, the enzymes are too cold to activate, so when you take them out to chop them up, it shouldn't make you cry. Also, cooking the onion gets rid of the enzymes.

Something else that changes when you heat it up is meat. The reason it does this is because, when it is raw, the molecules that make up the meat are wound up in tight coils. Heat the meat, and the tight bonds that were keeping the molecules wound up get broken and they unwind. It's this process that changes the colour of the meat and makes it nicer to eat.

If You Liked That, Try This

- The pizza sauce on page 23 makes a good meat-free pasta sauce, and you can adapt it in a number of ways.
- You can include almost any vegetables you like by adding them to the hot oil and cooking for a few minutes before the tomatoes go in. If you prefer your sauce without lumps, you can blend it once it's cooked, but leave it to cool a little first.
- You can also add different herbs or spices, or ham, pre-cooked bacon or tuna. These are already cooked so can be added at the end.

Quick Pesto

This is an easy homemade, versatile sauce that goes with pretty much anything except ice cream. You don't need very much as it's very flavoursome. If you're having it on hot pasta, put the pasta back in the saucepan once you've drained it, and stir the pesto in. You'll need a food processor, so ask an adult to help you if necessary.

What You'll Need

- 50g basil leaves (this will look like a lot)
- 30g pine nuts
- 30g Parmesan cheese, freshly grated
- 1 clove garlic, peeled and crushed
- 85ml olive oil
- Salt and freshly ground black pepper

1. Put the basil, parmesan, garlic and pine nuts into a food processor.

2. Whizz together and, with the motor still running, pour the oil in until the pesto thickens.

3. Taste the pesto and season it until you think it tastes good.

4. If you don't want to use it all straight away, store it in a clean jar in the fridge covered with a teaspoon of oil to prevent it drying out.

To check if spaghetti is cooked, throw a strand at the wall. If it sticks, it's done.

Just ONE strand, Dan!

Maybe you should use a timer instead?

Burger and Wedges
Makes enough for four people

What You'll Need
For the wedges:
- 3 large potatoes (or peeled sweet potatoes)
- 3 tablespoons oil
- Optional: salt and freshly ground black pepper

For the burgers:
- Half an onion or more, depending on how much you like onion
- 1 egg (you only need the yolk – see overleaf for how to separate it)
- 500g minced beef
- Salt and freshly ground black pepper
- Burger buns and salad, to serve

Equipment
- A sharp knife
- A chopping board
- A roasting tin
- A small bowl
- A mixing bowl
- A wooden spoon

To make the wedges:

1. Preheat the oven to 200°C/gas mark 6.

2. Cut each spud lengthways into around eight wedges. Put them in a bowl, add the oil and season with salt and pepper. Mix well, lay on a baking tray in a single layer and pop them in the oven for about 30 minutes. Ask a grown-up helper to turn them over halfway through.

To make the burgers:

1. Preheat the grill to medium.

2. Chop the onion into small bits – the smaller the better.

3. Separate the egg by cracking it open carefully over a small bowl, holding it upright so the yolk doesn't fall out. Let the white drip into the bowl as you gently tip the yolk from one half of the eggshell to the other. It's easy – see above. Even a chicken can do it. Save the

egg white to make Baked Alaska for pudding (see page 47).

4. Now mix the minced beef, onion and egg yolk together, with a little salt and pepper, until it all starts to hold together. Roll out four balls with your hands, and flatten them so they look like burgers.

5. Pop them under the grill. Now make sure you wash your hands. Cook the burgers for ten minutes on one side and then turn them over to cook for ten minutes on the other side.

6. Serve the burgers in buns with some salad and of course your delicious wedges on the side.

The Science Bit

Eggs bind things together because they coagulate when cooked. Yeah, we said coagulate, which means it goes from being a liquid into a semi-solid state, which helps to hold things together.

Quite tasty then, I'm guessing

If You Liked That, Try This

- You can add other stuff to the burger mix. Try some chopped herbs, or a little blue cheese – crumble it up into little lumps and it will melt when cooked.
- If some people don't like lumps of onion, you can grate the onion instead. It goes all mushy and smooth, so no one can tell it's there in the burger.
- Instead of burgers, roll 16 small balls. Fry them gently, and serve with pasta sauce and spaghetti.
- Do you think carrot or parsnip wedges would work?

Stir-fry

Stir-fries are so-called because you stir them while they fry. It's not rocket science. Makes enough for four people.

What You'll Need
- A selection of vegetables, such as:
- 1 red pepper
- 1 yellow pepper
- 100g broccoli florets
- 100g baby sweetcorn
- 100g mangetout
- 2 courgettes
- 50g water chestnuts (you'll find these in tins with the canned veg or with other Chinese ingredients)
- 1 clove garlic
- 2 tablespoons vegetable oil
- 2 tablespoons soy sauce

Stir-fries are healthier than other kinds of frying because you only use a small amount of oil, and the cut-up food cooks very quickly, which preserves more of the good stuff in it.

Equipment
- Sharp knives for chopping
- A chopping board
- A garlic crusher or small grater
- A big frying pan or wok
- A wooden spoon or spatula

Serve this with rice if you like, but we prefer noodles, especially fresh ones that we can cook in the wok with the vegetables. Follow the instructions on the packet. Packets can be useful like that. If you're having rice, start cooking it before you cut up all your vegetables as it takes longer to cook, but remember to set a timer.

1. Wash all your veg and chop it carefully so that all the pieces are about the same size. Peel and crush or grate the garlic.

2. Add the oil to a wok or a big frying pan. Once it is nice and hot, add all the vegetables and then stir them while you fry them. This should take you about five minutes. It is easier if only one person does the stirring.

3. Add a little soy sauce to make it tasty.

4. Serve the stir fried veg with the noodles or rice for a tasty meal.

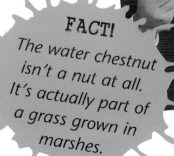

FACT!
The water chestnut isn't a nut at all. It's actually part of a grass grown in marshes.

Chicken Casserole

Makes enough for four people. You'll need chicken. Oh no, not that chicken again!

That has got to be the weirdest-looking chicken in the entire world

What You'll Need
- 500g chicken breast cut into bite-sized pieces
- Half an onion
- 2 sticks of celery, cut into large chunks
- 2 carrots, cut into large chunks
- 2 large potatoes
- 6 stalks of fresh thyme (or a tablespoon of dried thyme, but it won't be as tasty)
- 2 tablespoons olive oil
- 500ml stock (chicken or vegetable – mix according to the instructions on the packet)
- 2 teaspoons cornflour
- Salt and freshly ground black pepper

Equipment
- Knives for chopping
- A chopping board
- A big frying pan
- A spatula or a wooden spoon
- A plate
- A casserole dish (this is a dish that has a lid and can go in the oven)

1. Preheat the oven to 180°C/gas mark 4.

2. Cut the chicken breast into bite-sized pieces, chop the onion, celery, carrots and potatoes into large chunks and tear the thyme leaves off the stalks.

3. Put the oil in the frying pan and heat it on a medium heat on the hob. Once it is hot, put the pieces of chicken in and brown them all over. Lift them carefully on to a plate. Now put all the veg in the pan and fry it gently for about five minutes, stirring occasionally.

4. Take the pan off the heat, and put all the veg and the chicken in the casserole dish. Add the stock, a large pinch of mixed herbs and some salt and pepper.

5. Pop the dish in the oven for an hour or so with the lid on, and you'll have a tasty casserole.

If You Liked That, Try This

- Want a thicker sauce? Make a paste with a spoonful of the liquid and a little flour or cornflour, and stir it in before it goes in the oven.
- You could turn this into some small pies, or one large one, by spooning the mixture into a pie dish and using some bought pastry to make a lid.

The Science Bit

Cornflour is made up of lots and lots of tiny particles of starch, which when added to liquid makes it a bit thicker by hanging in it and allowing the liquid to pass around the particles. You can do really cool stuff with cornflour, but to find out what you'll have to check out a book called *Do Try This at Home*, also published by Macmillan.

Baked Salmon

This dish is so easy you'll think there's something a bit fishy about it . . .

What You'll Need
- Salmon steaks (skinless and boneless) – 1 per person or half each if you don't have a big appetite
- 1 clove garlic
- 1 lemon
- Olive oil
- Salt and freshly ground black pepper
- Fresh herbs such as parsley, dill or rosemary
- Some veg to serve with it – boiled potatoes and whatever you like

Equipment
- A baking tray
- Foil
- A garlic crusher or small grater
- A sharp knife
- A chopping board
- A fish slice

 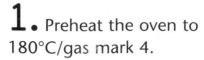

1. Preheat the oven to 180°C/gas mark 4.

2. Put some foil on a baking tray, and place your salmon steak on it.

3. Chop the garlic and slice the lemon.

4. Pour a drop of oil over the salmon. Sprinkle on salt and chuck the garlic and lemons on, then wrap the whole lot up in the foil to make a loose parcel. Put the baking tray with your salmon parcel on it in the oven.

5. While it's cooking, you can prepare your other veg.

6. After about 20–25 minutes take the salmon out of the oven and unwrap it. Make sure you take a big sniff because it smells delicious (but be careful of the hot steam!). Use a fish slice to transfer the salmon carefully on to plates with the vegetables.

The Science Bit

Oily fish, such as salmon, mackerel, sardines, trout and herring, are rich in omega-3 fatty acids, which help prevent heart disease and cancer, and are essential for brain development. It's also a good source of vitamins A and D, so make sure you eat some regularly!

You can wrap almost anything in foil.

If You Liked That, Try This

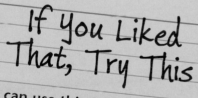

- You can use this foil method to cook other things too – try some cod or chicken with your choice of herbs instead.
- Serve with boiled new potatoes and a green salad for a delicious summery supper.

Smoothies

At Punk Science we like to think we're smooth, but none of us are as smooth as these rather delicious smoothies. Now THAT'S smooth.

Enough for one person

What You'll Need
● 1 banana
● 100g selection of berries – fresh or frozen
● 50g plain yogurt

Equipment
● A blender
● A glass

1. You can make a smoothie with pretty much any fruits, it just depends what you fancy, but this time we have gone for a banana, raspberries, blueberries, blackberries added to plain yogurt.

2. Pop everything in a blender and whizz it up. Then pour it into a glass for a refreshingly gloopy drink. You can add some fruit juice too if you want it to be less thick.

Lemonade

If you're thirsty after all this cooking, here's a great way to refresh your taste buds.

What You'll Need

- 4 unwaxed lemons, washed
- 100g caster sugar
- 1 litre water or sparkling water if you want your lemonade to be fizzy
- Ice

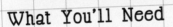

Equipment

- A sharp knife
- A chopping board
- You can squeeze the lemons by hand, but it's easier, and you'll probably get more juice out, if you use some kind of lemon squeezer
- A bowl
- A teaspoon
- A jug
- A spoon

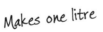
Makes one litre

1. Wash the lemons, cut them in half and squeeze out as much juice as you can into a bowl. Pick out the pips with a teaspoon.

2. Then simply mix together the sugar, lemon and water in a jug and stir until the sugar has dissolved. Pour yourself a glass of it, add some ice and you've got yourself lemonade.

You can use these drinks to make some fantastic ice lollies too. Just pour them into ice-lolly moulds and leave overnight. Amazing on a hot day, if you eat them before they melt.

Fruit Salad

Fancy a fruity treat? This easy-peasy recipe makes enough for four people.

What's yellow and sneaks up on you?
A lemon surprise.

What You'll Need
A selection of fruit, such as:
- 2 oranges
- A punnet of strawberries
- A punnet of raspberries
- Some fresh pineapple, or a tin of pineapple
- 2 kiwi fruit
- 2 apples
- Lemon juice or orange juice
- Optional: cream or yogurt

Equipment
- Sharp knives
- A chopping board
- A large bowl, or skewers and a griddle pan or frying pan

It tastes better if you chop the fruit up, Dan.

1. Wash your fruit, peel as necessary and chop it into chunks.

2. Take all the lovely chopped-up fruit and put it in a bowl. Add some orange juice, if you want to keep it in the fridge, as this will help to stop the fruit from going brown. Serve it with some cream or yogurt, if you like.

We said put FRUIT on to the skewers, not whatever that nonsense is . . . idiots!

If You Liked That, Try This

● You can use the fruit salad to make some kebabs to go on the barbecue:
1. Slot a selection of pieces of fruit on to each skewer.
2. Ask a grown-up helper to put the fruit skewers on to a hot griddle pan or barbecue. Turn them occasionally until they're cooked on all sides.

Summer Pudding

You don't just have to have this pudding in the summer, but it is better because that's when the fruits are fresh.

What do you bake in the garden?
Mud pie.

What You'll Need
- 6 slices of thick-cut bread
- 150g strawberries
- 150g blackberries
- 150g raspberries
- 100g caster sugar
- 100ml water

Equipment
- A knife
- A chopping board
- A saucepan
- A wooden spoon
- A medium bowl
- Cling film
- A saucer
- A weight, e.g. a jar of jam

The bread acts as a sponge, soaking up all that tasty berry juice.

You can make summer pudding Dan's way, but it is not recommended.

1. Cut each slice of bread into three rectangular strips.

2. Add the summer berries, sugar and water to a saucepan over a medium heat. Stir it occasionally until it gets syrupy and a bit gloopy. That's when it's ready.

3. Take a bowl and line it with cling film. Then dunk your bread bits into the berry mix and line the bowl with juicy bread, making sure there are no gaps. Leave some bits of bread spare for the top.

4. Pour the berry mix into the bowl so it is nearly full and place on the last few pieces of bread to cover up the top. Then put a saucer on top to help seal it up, and something heavy like a jar of jam on top of that. Put it in the fridge overnight to set.

5. When you are ready to eat it, get it out, place it upside down on a plate and ease your pudding out. The cling film will help. Sweet!

American Pancakes

You don't need to be American to make these, but it can help. At least, that's what Brad thinks.

Americans serve pancakes in a stack, like this.

What You'll Need
- 100g self-raising flour
- 1 egg
- 300ml milk
- Oil

Toppings:
- Maple syrup
- Sugar
- Lemon
- Berries

Equipment
- A mixing bowl
- A wooden spoon
- A small bowl
- A whisk
- A frying pan
- A spatula

⚠🔥 ⚠👨‍👧 ⚠2 (25 mins)

1. Have your toppings ready first, as you'll want to eat these pancakes as soon as they're done.

2. Put the flour in the mixing bowl. Beat the egg and mix it into the milk and pour that into the bowl too, a bit at a time, and mix some more. It should be nice and thick, a bit like Brad. It's now called batter and is ready for cooking.

3. Heat a small amount of oil in a frying pan on a medium heat and pour in a smallish circle of the batter. Cook it for a couple of minutes until it looks set (not liquid). Turn it over and cook on the other side, then remove from the pan.

4. Keep cooking more pancakes until all the batter is used up.

5. Enjoy your pancakes with maple syrup, lemon juice and sugar, berries or even flags. But don't eat the flags, as some countries might see this as an act of war.

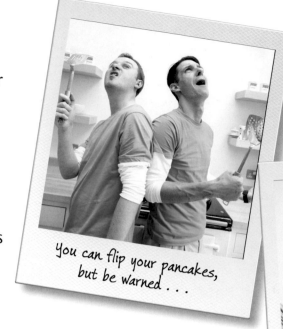

You can flip your pancakes, but be warned . . .

. . . it doesn't always go well, as Brad discovered.

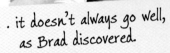

The Science Bit

A mixture of flour and milk (or water) is either called a dough or a batter, depending on how much of each ingredient there is. When it's cooked, batter turns from a liquid to a solid structure because starch granules in the flour absorb liquid and swell, creating a sponge-like network with millions of tiny air pockets.

Baked Alaska

Makes enough for four people. You can make one big one, or a small one each.

Alaska is a cold place in America. Yes, Brad – your country.

What You'll Need

- 1 Madeira or plain sponge cake, sliced in half horizontally. If you're making individual ones, cut each half into quarters
- 1 tub of vanilla ice cream
- 3 egg whites (separated from the yolks as in the burger recipe on page 30. This time you just need the whites. This recipe won't work if you get ANY yolk in with the egg white, so it's best to break each one into a separate bowl, just in case)
- 100g caster sugar

Equipment

- A baking tray
- An ice-cream scoop (optional)
- 3 small bowls
- A mixing bowl
- Whisk – electric or hand
- A spatula or spoon

    45 mins

1. Preheat the oven to 200°C/gas mark 6.

2. Place the bottom half of the cake on a baking tray, put a blob of ice cream on it and top with the rest of the cake, so you have a big ice cream sandwich (or four small ones).

3. Place the ice cream sandwiches in the freezer while you make the meringue mixture.

4. To make the meringue, whisk the egg whites in the mixing bowl until they form stiff peaks. They'll get so stiff they won't fall out even if you tip the bowl upside down! Then add the sugar one tablespoon at a time, stirring as you go, until you have a thick, glossy mixture.

5. Remove the ice cream sandwiches from the freezer and top with the meringue. Make sure to seal it all the way round – that's what stops the heat getting to the ice cream.

6. Put the whole lot in the oven and cook for five to ten minutes, making sure you keep an eye out so that it doesn't get burnt.

7. Serve immediately.

The Science Bit

This pudding works because the meringue acts as an insulator. An insulator is something that keeps warm things warm and cold things cold by preventing warm air from moving towards colder air. When we whisk the eggs to make the meringue, we create lots of tiny little air pockets that act as insulators. All this means is that even though the temperature is hot enough to cook the meringue on the outside, that heat cannot make it through the insulation to where the ice cream is, which is why it stays cold. Magic!

Jelly

You can pretty much put anything in jelly; you could even put stuff in it that might frighten another, weaker, Punk Scientist.

Probably best not to eat this kind of jelly – it might bite back.

What You'll Need

- 1 pack of jelly cubes – any flavour. We like orange best
- Boiling water
- Fruit – it's up to you what you use. We used a couple of satsumas

Equipment

- A measuring jug
- A jelly mould
- Optional: a sharp knife and chopping board, depending on what fruit you use

1. Make the jelly according to the instructions on the packet.

2. Allow it to cool down a bit and pour into the mould.

3. Chop some fruit and place it in the jelly.

4. Put the jelly in the fridge for at least two hours or overnight so it sets.

5. Run the tip of a sharp knife around the edge of the jelly. Then put a plate upside down over the mould and, holding tightly, turn the whole thing quickly right side up. Lift the mould and . . . mmmm, wobbly.

Too much jelly makes you wobbly too!

The Science Bit

Most of the gelatine that we use comes from the collagen in pig skin, although some comes from cattle skin and bones. Yum! Vegetarian versions are also available, but don't always work as well. Some fruits – including papaya, pineapple, melons and kiwi – contain enzymes that break up gelatine chains and stop jellies setting. You can still use these fruits in jellies though, as long as you cook them briefly first to deactivate the enzymes – or use tinned fruit, which has already been heated.

S'gone

Scones are a really easy bit of baking. In fact, this was the first thing to be produced in the Punk Science kitchen that wasn't just a mess and didn't taste of mud.

As in, you eat it and it's s'gone

What You'll Need

- 55g butter
- 225g self-raising flour, plus a bit extra for rolling out on
- 40g caster sugar
- 150ml milk
- 1 large egg
- Serve with butter, jam and whipped cream

Equipment

- A sieve
- A mixing bowl
- A knife
- A rolling pin
- A medium-sized pastry cutter
- A baking tray

1. Take the butter out of the fridge and preheat the oven to 220°C/gas mark 7.

2. Sift the flour into a mixing bowl.

3. Add the butter in smallish chunks. Now look at your hands. Are they clean? Or do they have gungy green stuff and mushrooms growing on them? If they do, give them a wash because you need to shove your hands into the bowl and rub the butter into the flour until your mixture looks like fine breadcrumbs.

4. Add the sugar, beaten egg and milk and mix until you get a dough that will stick together in a smooth ball.

5. Sprinkle some flour on a clean surface and tip the mixture on to it. Use

a rolling pin to smooth it out a bit. Not too much, though, as you want it to be quite thick, approximately two fingers high.

6. Use the cutter to cut out your scone shapes. Re-roll any extra dough and cut until you've used it all. You should get about eight or ten scones. Put them on a baking tray, then carefully put them in the oven.

7. They'll take about 15–20 minutes to bake. You'll know when they are done because they'll rise and go golden brown. If you're still not sure, once

you've taken them out of the oven, tap the bottom of one of the scones. If it sounds hollow it's definitely done; if it doesn't, it needs a bit longer. Eat as soon as they've cooled down.

The Science Bit

Self-raising flour contains baking powder. Baking powder works because it is made up of an acid and alkali that only mix together when it gets wet and hot. Once the acid and the alkali mix together, they react with each other and produce little bubbles of carbon dioxide, which push the scones upwards and outwards and make them rise.

Flapjacks

Oats are really good for you, which makes these flapjacks a healthy treat. Just ignore the butter. And the sugar. And the syrup. Oh dear . . .

What You'll Need
- 100g butter
- 50g caster sugar
- 75g golden syrup
- 200g oats

Equipment
- A shallow-sided baking tray
- Greaseproof paper
- A small saucepan
- A mixing bowl
- A wooden spoon
- A knife

1. Preheat the oven to 200°C/gas mark 6 and line a baking tray with greaseproof paper.

2. Put the butter, sugar and syrup in the saucepan and heat gently until they're melted.

3. Place all the ingredients in the bowl and mix together well.

4. Plop the mixture on to the baking tray, spread it out a bit with a knife and pop it in the oven to bake for 10–15 minutes.

5. Remove from the oven and leave to cool for five minutes.

6. Carefully cut the flapjack into little squares and get stuck in.

If You Liked That, Try This

- Add other things to the flapjack mix: sunflower seeds, sesame seeds, branflakes, etc.
- You could also try adding things to make them sweeter – chopped dried apricots, raisins, chocolate chips or chopped dried dates, for example.
- For a real treat, drizzle some melted chocolate over the flapjacks before you cut them into squares.

Bread

Nothing smells or tastes better than freshly baked, homemade bread. Delish!

Equipment
- A large mixing bowl
- A wooden spoon
- A 500g loaf tin
- Cling film

What You'll Need
- 325g bread flour, plus a little extra for kneading (bread flour is also called strong or very strong flour. You can use white, wholemeal or a mixture of both. The more wholemeal you use, the healthier, but more than half wholemeal makes a very dense, solid loaf)
- 1 sachet (7g) fast-action dried yeast
- 15g soft butter
- 1 teaspoon sugar
- 1 teaspoon salt
- 200ml water – 100ml cold, 100ml freshly boiled (use an extra 10ml of water if you're using any wholemeal flour)
- 1 teaspoon oil
- Optional: 1 egg and seeds (e.g. sunflower, pumpkin, poppy)

1. Put the flour into a bowl and add the yeast, butter, sugar and salt and mix together with clean hands or a wooden spoon.

2. Now mix the tepid water with the cold in a measuring jug and add to the flour mixture. Mix it in with your hands. It will be very sticky at first, but after a minute or so will start to form a smooth ball of dough. If it's still very sticky, add a little more flour, a tablespoon at a time.

3. Sprinkle flour on a clean work surface and knead the dough for ten minutes until it becomes elastic and springs back when prodded.

4. Grease the bread tin and put the dough in.

5. Cover the tin with cling film and leave it in a warm, dry place to rise. You want the dough to be getting on for double the size it was, which will probably take 30–45 minutes.

6. Preheat the oven to 230°C/gas mark 8.

7. Once the dough has risen, if you would like your finished loaf to have a seedy top, brush the surface lightly with egg and sprinkle seeds all over it – we like poppy, sunflower or pumpkin seeds or a combination. Pop the loaf in the oven to bake for 30 minutes.

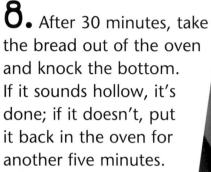

See the 'Awaken the Yeast' experiment on page 66 to discover what's going on inside the dough.

8. After 30 minutes, take the bread out of the oven and knock the bottom. If it sounds hollow, it's done; if it doesn't, put it back in the oven for another five minutes.

9. Leave your bread to cool for five minutes, then tip it out of the tin and leave to cool completely on a cooling rack.

If You Liked That, Try This:

You can divide your dough into rolls instead if you like. They will cook in 15–20 minutes.

Punky Cakes

Because sometimes even punks need a cakey treat

Why are bakers rich? Because they've got plenty of dough.

Makes about 15

What You'll Need

For the cakes:

- 125g soft butter (take it out of the fridge about an hour beforehand)
- 125g sugar
- 2 medium eggs
- 125g self-raising flour

For the icing:

- 125g icing sugar
- 1 tablespoon warm water or lemon juice (for lemony icing)
  Optional:
- Food colourings
- Other toppings: small sweets, cake decorations, chocolate drops, glacé cherries

Equipment

- A mixing bowl
- A wooden spoon
- 2 or more small bowls
- A sieve
- Paper cake cases
- A cupcake/muffin baking tin
- A rubber spatula
- A cake rack
- Small bowls for icing
- Spoons for mixing
- A knife

⚠️🔥 ⚠️2 ⏱45 mins

1. Preheat the oven to 200°C/gas mark 6.

2. Put the butter and sugar into a mixing bowl and mix with a wooden spoon until they are pale golden and smooth.

3. Crack the egg into a small bowl, beat it and add it to the butter mixture and mix.

4. Sift in the flour and mix gently.

5. More mixing. Keep at it until the mixture is quite soft and smooth.

6. Pop the paper cake cases into the cupcake baking tin and spoon the mixture into the cases. Use a rubber spatula to make sure you get all the cake mix out.

7. Pop the cakes into the oven to bake for 20 minutes. They should be risen and golden and springy to the touch. Leave them on a cake rack to cool.

8. When the cakes are cool, sift the icing into a bowl and stir in the lemon juice or water. It will be very stiff at first, but will become smooth as you mix it. If you need more liquid, add no more than a drop at a time.

If You Liked That, Try This:

- If you want to, you can split the icing into batches and stir different food colourings into each batch. With a spoon and a knife, spread the icing on the cakes quickly, before it sets. Once you have iced the cakes, decorate with any other toppings straight away, before the icing hardens. You could try small sweets, cherries or sprinkles.
- You can mix other things into the cake mixture before you fill the cases – nuts, raisins or chocolate chips would all be delicious.

Carrot Bars

You might not realize how delicious carrots can be in cakes. We didn't, which led to some confusion in our carrotty dessert efforts, as you can see to the right . . .

These look stupid and taste as bad as they look.

Fact!
Carrots weren't always orange. They used to be off-white or purple, but were grown orange to celebrate William of Orange coming to the British throne.

What You'll Need
- 175g soft butter (take it out of the fridge about an hour beforehand)
- 80g brown sugar
- 2 eggs
- 55g self-raising wholewheat flour
- 175g grated carrot

Equipment
- A 20cm-square cake tin
- Greaseproof paper
- A mixing bowl
- A wooden spoon
- A small bowl
- A fork or small whisk
- A tablespoon
- A knife

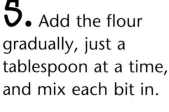

1. Preheat the oven to 180°C/gas mark 4.

2. Line the baking tray with greaseproof paper.

3. Mix the butter and sugar together in the mixing bowl.

4. Crack the eggs one at a time into a small bowl and beat. Then add to the mixture and beat in.

5. Add the flour gradually, just a tablespoon at a time, and mix each bit in.

6. Add the grated carrot and stir.

7. Place the mixture in the lined baking tray, spread it out and bake for 40 minutes.

8. Leave to cool before cutting into bars.

If You Liked That, Try This:

- All sorts of vegetables can be used to make yummy sweet treats . . .
- Courgette cake, chocolate and beetroot cake, pumpkin date cake and potato ginger cake are all totally delicious!

The Science Bit

Wholegrain foods contain more fibre and other nutrients than white or refined starchy foods. We also digest wholegrain foods more slowly, so they can help make us feel full for longer.

Cheesecake

No, not a cake made of brie, or Cheddar. We're not crazy. Yet.

What You'll Need

- 10 x digestive biscuits
- 50g butter
- 200g mascarpone (a type of creamy Italian cheese)
- 200g soft cream cheese
- 200ml whipping cream
- 2 tbs icing sugar
- 2 lemons
- Topping of your choice, e.g. 100g blueberries

Equipment

- A plastic freezer bag
- A rolling pin
- A saucepan
- A spoon
- A very fine grater
- 2 small bowls
- A lemon squeezer (optional)
- A mixing bowl
- A whisk – hand or electric
- A 20cm cake tin with removable base
- A sharp knife

Not that kind of cheese!

Biscuit fu – effective, but very messy

Not effective AND very messy

Much more sensible!

1. Crush the biscuits into small pieces. We put them into a sealed plastic freezer bag, careful to squash out as much air as possible, and smashed them up using a rolling pin.

2. Melt the butter over a gentle heat. Pour in the biscuit crumbs and stir until you have a crumbly rubble.

3. Put the mixture into the cake tin and press it down to make a firm base. Pop the tin into the fridge so that the mixture can set.

4. Wash the lemons and grate the outside skin, called the zest. Then cut the lemons in half and squeeze out as much juice as you can, removing any pips with a teaspoon. Put the zest and juice aside to use soon.

5. Now for the cheesy bit. Pour the cream into the bowl and whisk it until it forms soft peaks. Mix in the mascarpone, soft cheese, icing sugar and add the lemon juice and grated lemon zest. Rather than add it all at once, you might want to add half and taste it to see if you need to add more.

6. Spoon the cheese mixture into the tin, making sure it's all level, and put whatever you like on top. We've gone for blueberries.

7. Pop it into the fridge to set for a couple of hours.

8. Here's the tricky part: getting the cake out of the cake tin. Our tip is to run a sharp knife round the edge of the cake, then balance the cake on a big sturdy mug, unlock the catch on the tin (if there is one) and gently push the ring of the cake tin down. There's your cake, ready to slice and scoff – but take it off the mug first.

Awaken the Yeast

That's 'yeast', not 'beast'. If you know any beasts, best let them wake up in their own time.

What You'll Need

- A fizzy-drink bottle (has to be fizzy as they're designed to take a bit of pressure)
- Some yeast
- Some sugar
- Warm water
- A balloon
- A funnel
- A bowl
- A spoon

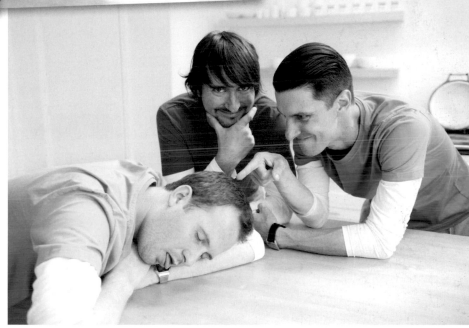

1. Put the yeast and sugar in the warm water and give it a stir.

2. Pour the mixture through the funnel into the fizzy-drink bottle.

3. Place the balloon over the top of the bottle.

4. Leave the bottle for between 30 minutes to an hour.

5. Watch carefully as the balloon slowly inflates with gas.

The Science Bit

The yeast is actually thousands of microscopic living plants that are activated by warm liquid and fed by sugar and starch.

When activated by the warm water, the now live yeast releases carbon dioxide gas bubbles. It's these bubbles that are inflating the balloon and they are also what make bread rise. Without yeast, bread would be as flat as a pancake.

Spud Spear

This is possibly the most simple experiment in the world, but it is without a doubt a Punk Science all-time favourite. When we first heard about this experiment, we didn't stop doing it for days.

What You'll Need
- A potato
- A straw
(It's THAT easy)

The perfect spear,
I think . . .

And my technique is
also spot-on . . .

Oh.

1. Get a potato and a straw.

2. Hold the potato in one hand and the straw in the other, making sure there are no bends or imperfections in the straw.

3. Using all your might, plunge the straw into the potato. The straw should go quite far in. With practise you should be able to get the straw to go the whole way through.

4. Try it again, but this time do it slowly. Shock! Horror! It doesn't work, but why not?

The Science Bit

The straw only goes through the potato when you use a lot of force because all that force is being applied evenly, making the straw a very strong structure. However, when you don't use much force, the structure of the straw is quite weak and imbalanced, which means the straw bends and flops all over the place and is generally rubbish as a potato-impaling device. Clever!

Cabbage Detector

Who needs Sherlock Holmes
or Hercule Poirot when
you've got a cabbage?
Not us. OK, maybe us.

What You'll Need
- Half a red cabbage
- A sharp knife
- A chopping board
- A saucepan
- A sieve
- A bowl
- 2 glasses
- Orange juice
- 1 tablespoon of flour

1. Chop up the cabbage and put it into the saucepan.

2. Stir the cabbage on a low heat until you see lots of purple juice coming out.

3. Drain the purple cabbage juice through a sieve into a bowl. You need to keep this juice, as it's what you'll be using for the experiment.

4. Now you can use the cabbage juice to see whether something is acid or alkali. Pour some cabbage juice into two glasses.

5. Add some orange juice to one of the glasses and see what colour it goes.

6. Now add some flour to the other glass of cabbage juice and see if it goes a different colour.

The Science Bit

If the cabbage juice goes red, then you have an acid. If it goes a lighter blue, then it's an alkali. This is because red cabbage contains something called anthocyanins that are pH sensitive, meaning that they change colour when they come into contact with acids or alkalis.

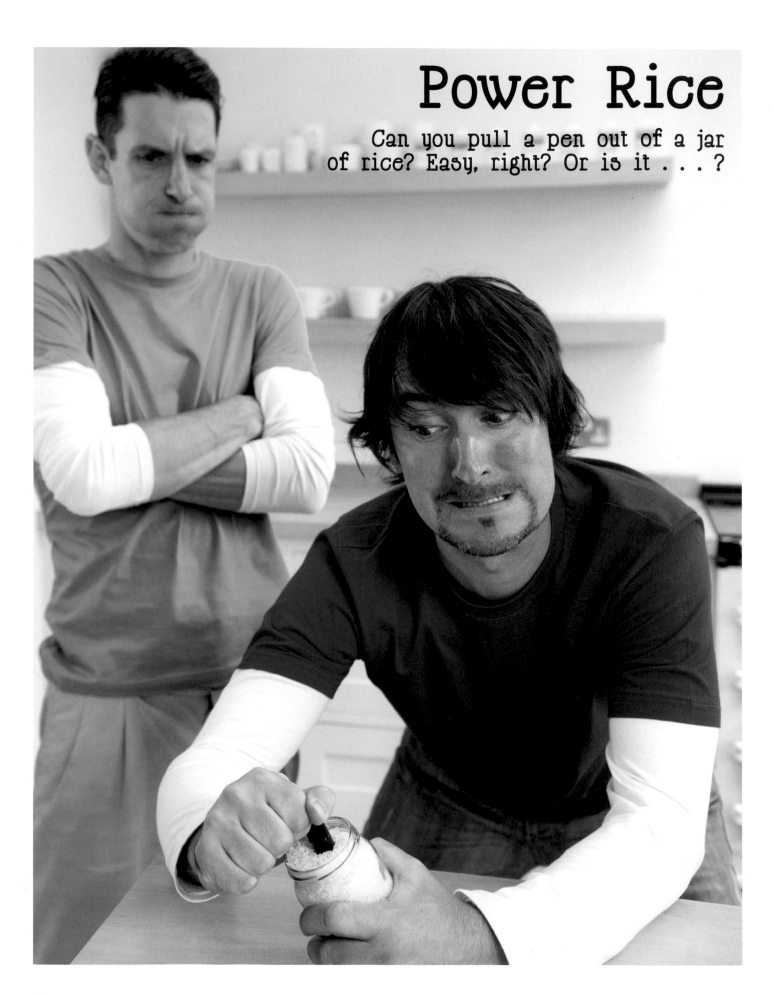

Power Rice

Can you pull a pen out of a jar
of rice? Easy, right? Or is it . . . ?

1. Fill your jar full of rice. Yes, right to the top, otherwise this won't work.

2. Now gently push your pen all the way to the bottom of the jar. This will take time and you will lose a bit of rice, so be patient.

3. Now get someone else to try to pull the pen out. They will find it quite difficult, and in some cases impossible.

The Science Bit

It's hard to pull the pen out not because the person is weak, but because collectively the rice is very strong. All those pieces of rice create loads of friction and, as we all know, friction is the force that slows things down. In this case it slows things down a *lot*, so it's really tough to get that pen out.

Rubber Egg

Use vinegar to make a bouncy egg.

What You'll Need
- A large glass
- 200ml white wine vinegar
- 1 egg

1. Pour the vinegar into a bowl and then put an egg into the bowl.

2. Cover the bowl with some cling film.

3. Leave the egg in there for at least 24 hours. Here's what we did while we were waiting (right).

4. Get the egg out of the vinegar and marvel at the fact that it is no longer hard like an egg normally is; it is now rubbery. You may even be able to bounce it!
It is probably best to try that outside, just in case!

The Science Bit

The shell of the egg has been broken down by the acid in the vinegar, which also 'cooks' the inside and makes it solid and rubbery. Eggs-cellent!

Eggs-pert

Here's another egg-speriment that you can do as a test on someone else.

1. First show a friend your two eggs. One has to be hard-boiled and the other has to be raw.

2. Get them to guess which egg they think is the hard-boiled egg. Then switch the eggs around behind your back just to make sure they don't know which is which.

3. Place both eggs on a surface and give them a spin – now ask them to guess which one is the hard-boiled one. You'll be able to tell which egg is which because the hard-boiled egg spins for much longer than the raw egg.

What You'll Need
- One hard-boiled egg
- One raw egg

Still spinning

Stopped straight away

The Science Bit

Inside the raw egg, the yolk and white are wobbly and move around as you spin it. This slows the egg down. In the hard-boiled egg, the solid yolk and white are held in place, as if they had little seatbelts on, and the egg isn't slowed down when it spins.

Sour Milk

Here's an experiment that may turn sour in more ways than one.

1. Squeeze a little lemon juice into a glass of milk.

2. You can see that the milk has curdled, but don't do what we've done and offer it to your friends to drink. They might not be your friends for much longer.

The Science Bit

Milk contains proteins that float around in it. When you add lemon juice, it makes the watery part of the milk acidic. The proteins really don't like this, so they gang up together so they have less surface area touching the now acidic, watery part of the milk. This is called curdling and a similar process is used when making cheese.

Celery Sucks

Ever wanted to eat red celery? No? Just us?

What You'll Need
- A large glass or vase
- Water
- Food colouring
- 1 stick of celery

1. Put some water into a glass or vase and add some food colouring.

2. Put the celery in the glass.

3. Look at the new colour of the celery! Ours has gone red.

The Science Bit

The celery sucks water up through itself to keep it healthy. This is called capillary action. So all that's happening here is that because we coloured the water red, we can see where it has been sucked up into the celery.

Our celery has come out like a heart shape, so you could give it to a loved one on their birthday or for Valentine's Day. But be warned: they will think you are odd.

Taste the Difference

Find out how important your nose is to your sense of taste.

What You'll Need

- A volunteer
- Nose clips (like the ones swimmers wear)
- A blindfold
- Mints

1. Fix the nose clips on the volunteer's nose, then put the blindfold on them too.

2. Pop a mint in the volunteer's mouth and they won't really taste anything.

3. Remove the nose plug and they should suddenly taste the mint in their mouth.

4. You can test this on yourself too, but obviously you won't need the blindfold! You can also try this with other foods if you like. Fancy a raw onion?

The Science Bit

The majority of our sense of taste actually comes through our noses. That's why you can't taste things well when you have a blocked-up nose from a cold.

Mmm, minty . . .

I love onions, me.

Guys, I'm ready to do the experiment. Guys? Hello?

Preservation

The thing about food is that it doesn't hang around. You grow it, you prepare it, you eat it and then you digest it, taking out what you need and letting the rest go, so to speak. But sometimes we want to keep food for longer, so we can have the lovely tastes and flavours all year round, when that particular type of food isn't in season. Some people say this isn't a particularly good idea because it means the food isn't fresh and it doesn't taste as good, but the process of preserving things is quite interesting so we thought we would tell you a bit about it.

The reason you need to preserve things is to stop the food from going bad, which can happen in a number of ways. Bacteria, fungi and all sorts of micro-organisms can grow on food if it's left for too long. Added to that, there's the problem of oxygen – yes, oxygen, the stuff we breathe. Oxygen actually damages food over time, so how do we stop all of this? Well, humans are ingenious creatures, and over the years we've come up with lots of different ways . . .

Burying
Yes, it sounds disgusting, and, no, it is not recommended for daily use, but burying your food is an ancient method for preserving it. It works due to the cooler temperature underground combined with a lack of oxygen, but all your food will taste a bit muddy.

Dehydration
Another really old way of preserving food is by drying it. Removing the water in the food means the bacteria don't have anything in which to grow, which means the food can last much longer.

Salting
An old method that also works by drawing the water out of the food is salting. Adding salt has been used for years but does make your food taste, well – salty. A bit of a drawback.

Pickling
The process of pickling can seem a bit of a pickle, but is actually quite easy. You take your food and plop it in a liquid that stops bacteria growing, such as vinegar or olive oil.

Preserving

Jams and jellies are great at preserving food too, and not just for fruits such as strawberries and oranges – it also works on meat. The process for each is a bit different, but it is essentially the same thing.

Canning

When food is canned, it is sealed so the air can't get to it, and then boiled to kill off any bacteria that might be hanging around.

Pasteurizing

Something else micro-organisms don't like is extreme heat, which is why they heat things like milk, in a process called pasteurization.

Freezing

This involves lowering the food's temperature, usually to about −18°C, which stops the germs growing as they don't like the cold.

Vacuum packing

More modern, high-tech methods rely on stopping the micro-organisms from getting air by removing it, as in vacuum packing.

Pickled Onions

What you'll need
- 1kg small pickling onions or shallots, peeled
- 30g salt
- 1 teaspoon dried chilli flakes
- 1 litre malt vinegar
- 180g granulated sugar
- Some clean jars with clean lids

1. Put the onions in a large bowl with the salt and mix together. Cover and leave overnight.

2. Rinse well in cold water and allow to dry as much as possible.

3. Pack the onions into the very clean jars. Push as many in as you possibly can.

4. Put the vinegar, chilli flakes and sugar into a pan and slowly bring to the boil to dissolve the sugar.

5. Pour the vinegar over the onions and put the lids on tightly. Store the jars in a cool, dark cupboard for two weeks before eating.

Cookery Terms

beat – a quick, hard mix with a fork, spoon or whisk, for example with eggs

bake – to cook in the oven

blend – to mix two or more ingredients so that they combine

boil – to heat water to 100°C. You will know it is boiling because there will be lots of big bubbles

brown – to cook something enough to change its colour

chop – this just means cutting things up. We tend to use a paring knife because it's not too big. Remember, if you are chopping anything you should always get a grown-up to help

cream – to mix two or more ingredients together, most commonly butter and sugar to make a cake

dice – to chop up into small cubes

fry – to cook on a hob, using a frying pan with oil in it

fold – a particular kind of gentle mixing where you scoop up some of the food with a spoon and turn it over the rest. We do it to make sure we don't squash out the trapped air in a meringue or cake mix, for instance

grate – to use a grater to cut food into lots of tiny strips. A grater has lots of holes with little blades. Be careful not to grate your fingers. Not trying to grate the very last bit of food can help

grease – to rub butter on something, for instance a cake tin before you add the cake mixture. This stops it sticking to the pan

knead – to fold dough and give it a push with the palms of your hands, over and over again, until it gets smooth and shiny

stock – a liquid made by cooking bones, meat, fish or vegetables in water, which is then used as the basis of soups or sauces

toss – to shake or turn food so as to mix it or coat it with something, such as a dressing or sauce

roll (out) – to squish pastry or dough flat, using a rolling pin

rub in – to combine butter and flour, usually with your fingers

season – to add salt and pepper to something

whisk – to mix air into something, usually done pretty quickly using a whisk (duh)

whip – a bit like whisking but harder and faster and more of it to put lots more air in the mixture. When you whip cream, it gets thicker

sift – to push something through a sieve to get rid of lumps, for instance flour

simmer – not quite as hot as boiling, with smaller bubbles

steam – to cook something using the steam from boiling water

Conversions

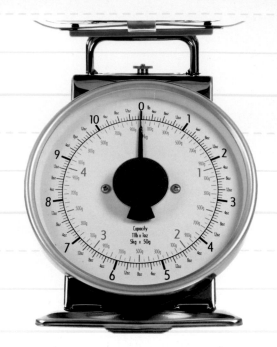

Here's where it can get a bit confusing, but don't worry because we Punk Scientists are here to help. There are two main different types of measurements. They are called metric and imperial. The metric system is the one you are more likely to know, but you'll probably also recognize some of the measurements from the imperial system, like a pint of liquid.

'Why do we need more than one system?' we hear you cry. Well, the truth is, we don't. It's just what we happen to have because different people created their own ways of measuring things and some people thought one method was good and others thought that a different one was best. It can leave you a bit flummoxed, so here is what you might need to know.

You'll find that recipes give metric measurements (as in this book) or imperial, or both versions. If it gives either, as long as you can weigh your ingredients according to the same system, you won't need to worry about how the two systems compare. If a recipe gives both, choose one – metric or imperial – and stick to it for the whole recipe.

Let's look at weights and measures first, which tell you how heavy something is or how much volume it has. We'll get on to temperature in a minute because that works on another set of systems.
So:

**1 gram = 0.035 ounces
1 kilogram = 2.2 pounds
1 litre = 1.76 pints**

And:

**1 ounce = 28.35 grams
1 pound = 0.45 kilograms
1 pint = 568 millilitres**

METRIC V. IMPERIAL
The most commonly used metric units for weighing and measuring ingredients are milligrams (mg), grams (g), kilograms (kg), millilitres (ml) and litres (l), whereas the imperial units are ounces (oz), pounds (lb) and pints (pt).

Temperature-wise it's a different story – it's all about degrees Celsius (°C), degrees Fahrenheit (°F) and, because we're talking about cooking, gas mark, as well. (Gas marks aren't a scale to measure temperature like the other two; it's just the settings used on a gas oven.)

Celsius is the most common form of measurement and the one we Punk Scientists use, but it's worth mentioning Fahrenheit too. Celsius was developed back in the eighteenth century by a Swedish scientist named Anders Celsius, hence the name. Fahrenheit was proposed in 1724 by Daniel Fahrenheit and works on a different scale to Celsius.

So the freezing point of water:
   0°Celsius = 32°Fahrenheit

And the boiling point of water:
   100°Celsius = 212°Fahrenheit

Gas ovens have their own scale, which corresponds to the Celsius scale as follows:
   Gas mark 1 = 140°C
   Gas mark 2 = 150°C
   Gas mark 3 = 160–170°C
   Gas mark 4 = 180°C
   Gas mark 5 = 190°C
   Gas mark 6 = 200°C
   Gas mark 7 = 220°C
   Gas mark 8 = 230°C

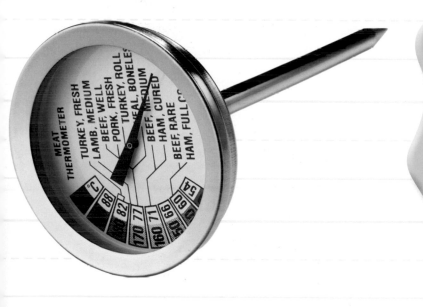

If that's not enough for you in the temperature stakes, look at Lord Kelvin, a Scottish physicist who came up with his own scale in 1848. The Kelvin scale starts at absolute zero, which is the coldest you can go and is really, really cold. Like, if you imagine the coldest you've ever been and times it by a thousand, it's that cold. 0°Kelvin is –273.15°Celsius. That's 273.15°C colder than the freezing point of water. Brrrrrrr!

Quick Quiz

Are you an egghead or a spudhead?

1. What's the boiling point of water?

2. How many times do you see one of the punks dressed as a chicken?

3. How many spoons are there in the entire book? (It can be the same spoon in different pictures.)

4. What makes you cry in onions?

5. Which punk is wrapped up in foil on page 37?

6. We showed you how to make baked Alaska, but which country is Alaska part of?

7. What creepy beast is in the jelly?

8. Who from history did we say ate baked dormice?

9. Can you use cheddar cheese to make cheesecake?

10. Look at page 5. How many spuds can you see? (*We* don't count.)

16. What colour is the balloon that scares Jon?

17. We made baked salmon, but which of these things can salmon do?
a. Jump up waterfalls
b. Wear jumpers
c. Knit jumpers

18. On page 15, what colour is the avocado express?

19. Are tomatoes vegetables?

20. How much do you enjoy food?
a. A bit
b. A lot
c. Not at all, I only bought this book to eat instead of food

11. Look for baked potatoes and work out what Dan is riding?

12. What is written on the fridge on page 27?

13. What punctuation mark did we make using pizza?

14. Is a water chestnut a nut?

15. What colour cabbage do we use to make our pH indicator?

Answers overleaf

Answers

1) 100° Celsius

2) 5, plus one glove puppet

3) 33

4) Sulphenic acid

5) Jon

6) The USA

7) A spider

8) The Romans

9) Yes, but it would be disgusting. So really it's a no

10) 10

11) A toy tractor

12) punk

13) A question mark

14) No, it's a type of grass

15) Red

16) Yellow

17) a. Jump up waterfalls

18) Green

19) No, they're fruit – see page 23

20) No real answer here, it's up to you – but eating books is probably a bad idea as the pages can get stuck in your teeth